The Czech Lute for Ukulele

by Adam Václav Michna z Otradovic

arranged

Ondřej Šárek

Contents

Introductions		3
1.	Foreword	4
2.	The Calling of a Spiritual Bride	5
3.	The Glorious Gift of the Mother of God	6
4.	Wedding Ring	8
5.	Virgin Love	10
6.	Farewell to the World	12
7.	Spiritual Wedding Purgation	14
8.	Spiritual Dowry	16
9.	Angel Friendship	18
10.	Bridal Wreath	19
11.	Wedding Day	20
12.	The Fight between the Soul and the Body	22
13.	The Grief of the Foolish Virgins	23

ISBN-13: 978-1481013192
ISBN-10: 148101319X

Introductions

Adam Václav Michna z Otradovic (1600 - 1676) Czech catholic aristocrat, poet, composer, hymn writer, organist and choir leader. He belongs among most important early Czech Baroque composers, who influenced subsequent artist generation.

Michna wrote and composed Czech Lute in 1653. It is the collection of 13 pieces. Although, we will play only tablature, it can seem to be the collection of dancing compositions at first sight. But the opposite is true. The song collection was written in Baroque era and Michna was not only a composer and a poet but mainly a believer. Each song has about 10 verses. Michna uses here Baroque poet imaginations and by singing and the lute he celebrates mystical marriage of the divine Bridegroom (Christ or God the Father) with a virgin bride – the Virgin Mary.

The original version was written for two singing voices and basso continuo.

I cannot forgive and quote recommendations where and how to play songs from the first issue of notes.

CZECH LUTE in the holiday, on Friday, at church, at table, as it likes, at any moment, joyfully, sadly, sounding saving

Score

Předmluva - 01

Foreword

Adam Václav Michna z Otradovic
arr: Ondřej Šárek

Score

Povolání duchovné nevěsty - 02

The Calling of a Spiritual Bride

Adam Václav Michna z Otradovic
arr: Ondřej Šárek

Moderato

Score

Matky Boží slavná nadání - 03

The Glorious Gift of the Mother of God

Adam Václav Michna z Otradovic

arr: Ondřej Šárek

Matky Boží slavná nadání

Svadební prstýnek - 04

Score

Wedding Ring

Adam Václav Michna z Otradovic
arr: Ondřej Šárek

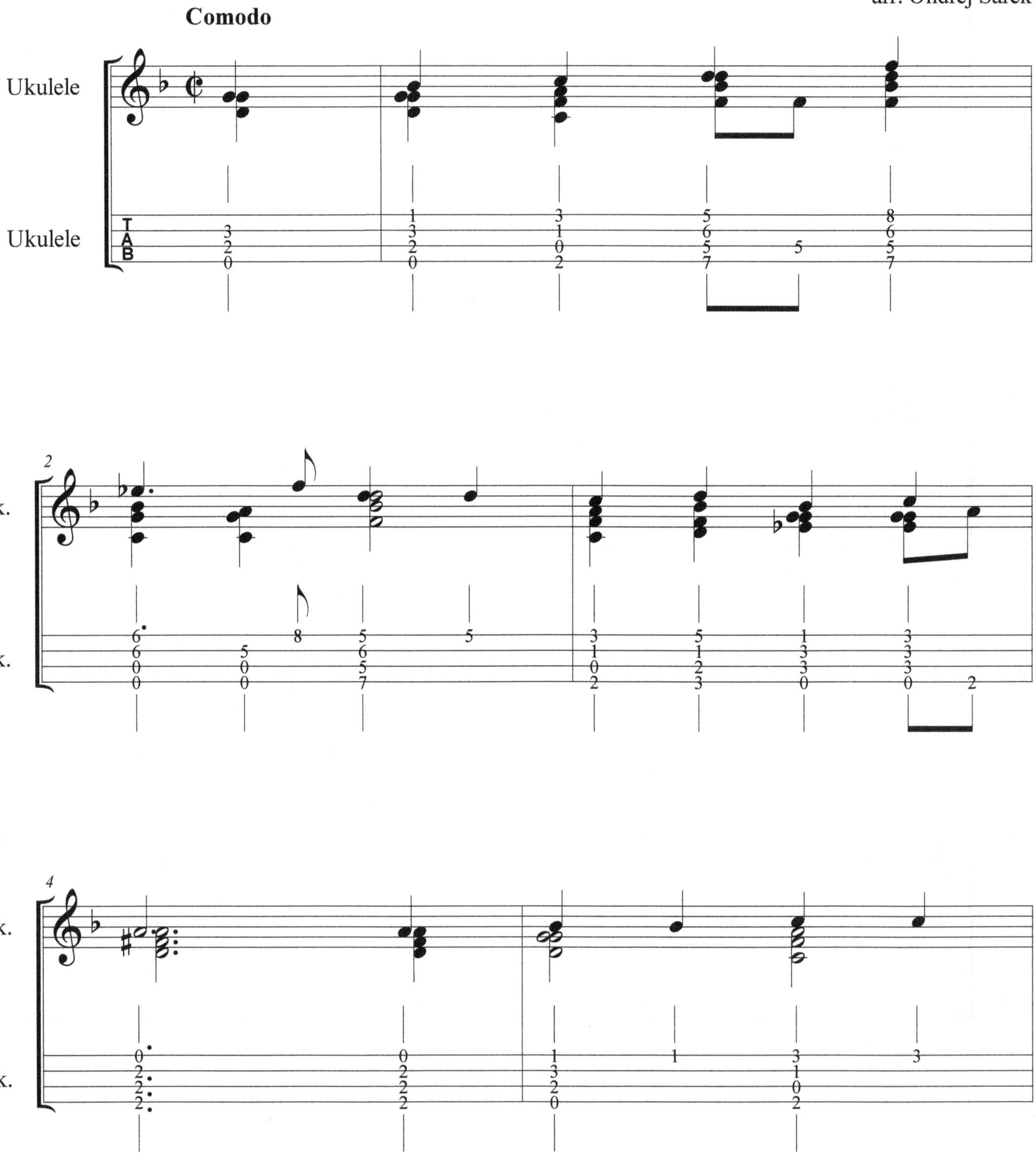

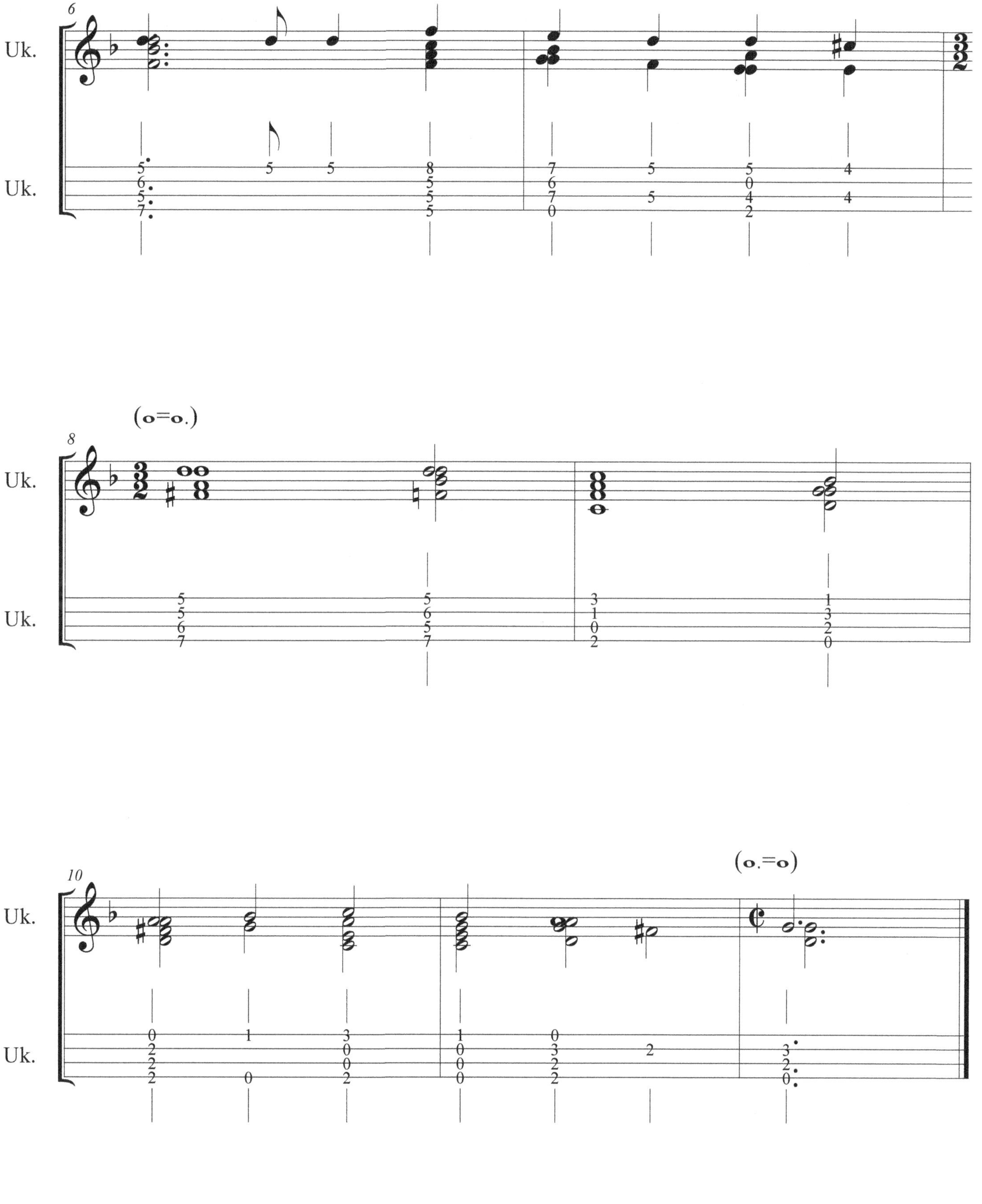
Uk.
Uk.

Score

Panenská láska - 05

Virgin Love

Adam Váslav Michna z Otradovic

arr: Ondřej Šárek

8
Uk.
Uk.
10
Uk.
Uk.
12
Uk.
Uk.

Score

Žehnání s světem - 06

Farewell to the World

Adam Václav Michna z Otradovic
arr: Ondřej Šárek

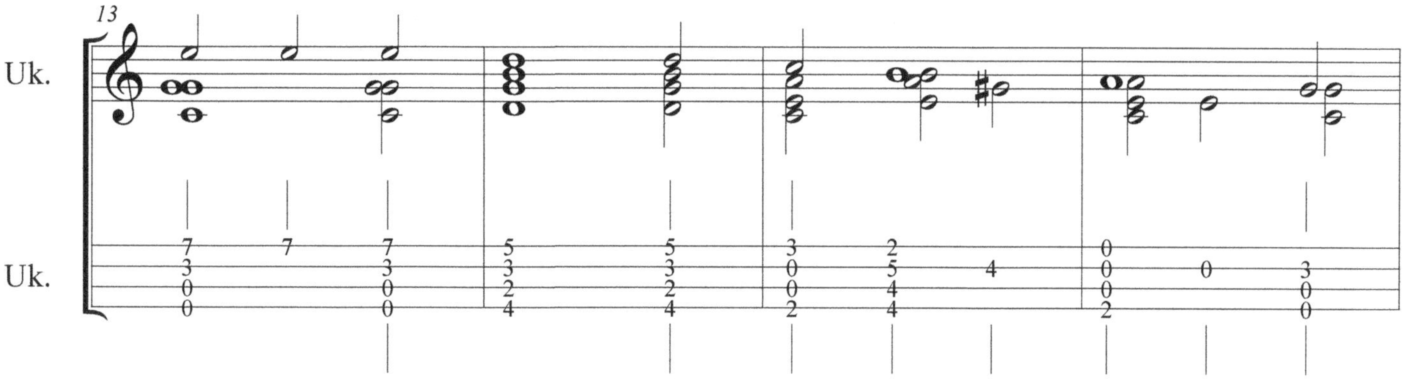
13
Uk.
Uk.

17
Uk.
Uk.

Score

Duchovní svadební lázeň - 07

Spiritual Wedding Purgation

Adam Václav Michna z Otradovic
arr: Ondřej Šárek

Animato

This page has been left blank to
avoid awkward page turns.

Score

Duší věno - 08

Spiritual Dowry

Adam Václav Michna z Otradovic
arr: Ondřej Šárek

9
Uk.
Uk.

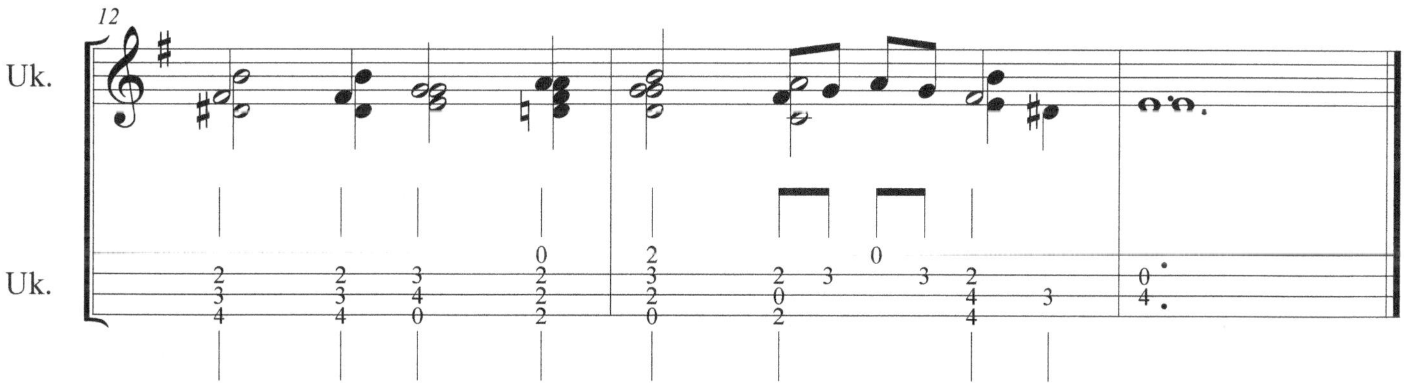
12
Uk.
Uk.

Score

Andělské přátelství - 09

Angel Friendship

Adam Václav Michna z Otradovic

arr: Ondřej Šárek

Allegro vivace

Score

Svadební věneček - 10

Bridal Wreath

Adam Václav Michna z Otradovic

arr: Ondřej Šárek

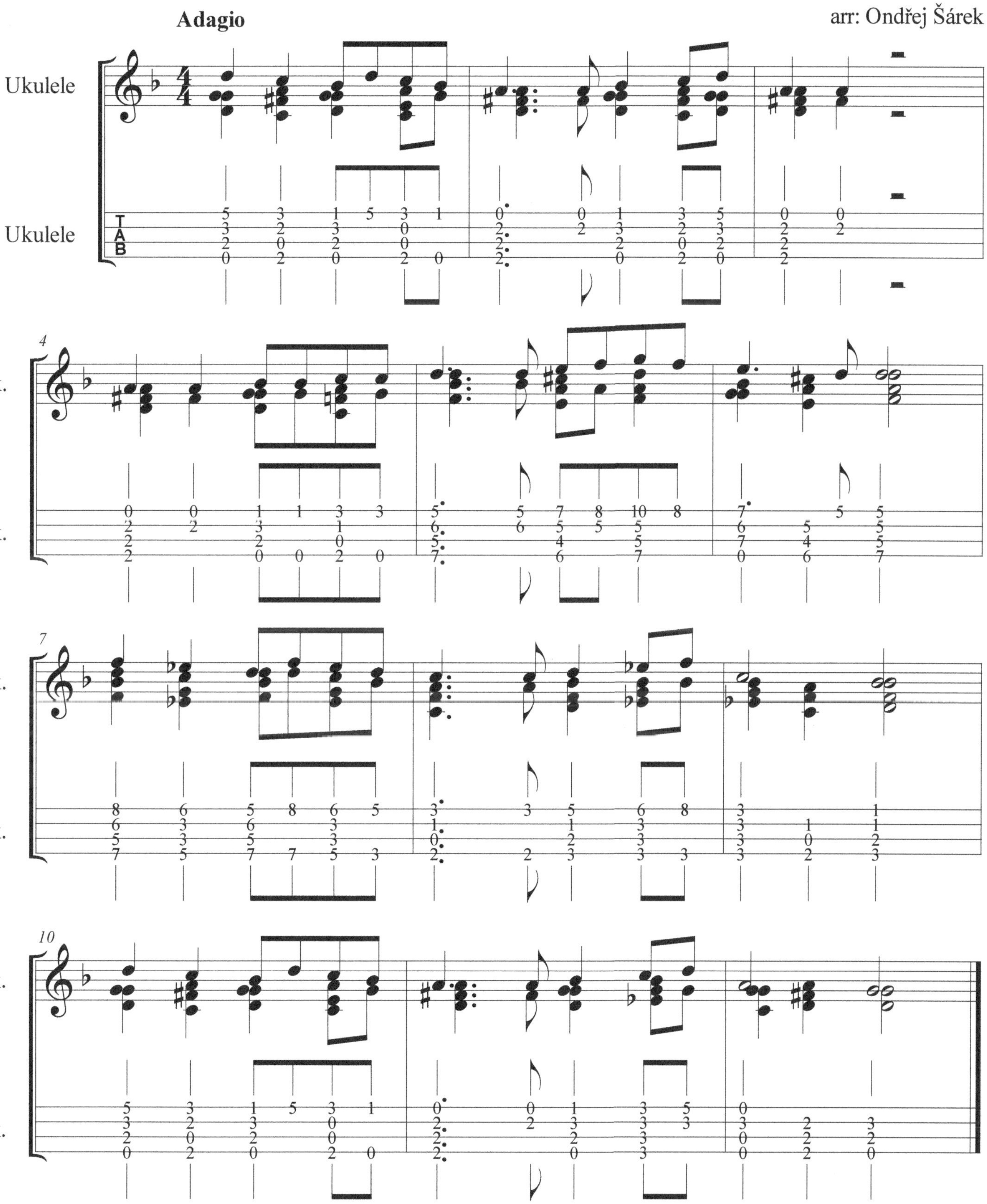

Den svadební - 11

Score

Wedding Day

Adam Václav Michna z Otradovic
arr: Ondřej Šárek

Allegro moderato

Uk.
Uk.

Score

Domácí vojna mezi duší a tělem - 12

The Fight between the Soul and the Body

Adam Václav Michna z Otradovic

arr: Ondřej Šárek

Score

Smutek bláznivých panen - 13

The Grief of the Foolish Virgins

Adam Václav Michna z Otradovic
arr: Ondřej Šárek

Allegro assai

New ukulele books

For C tuning ukulele
Classics for Ukulele (Mel Bay Publications)
Ukulele Bluegrass Solos (Mel Bay Publications)
Antonin Dvorak: Biblical Songs (CreateSpace Independent Publishing Platform)
Irish tunes for all ukulele (CreateSpace Independent Publishing Platform)
Gospel Ukulele Solos (CreateSpace Independent Publishing Platform)
Gregorian chant for Ukulele (CreateSpace Independent Publishing Platform)
The Czech Lute for Ukulele (CreateSpace Independent Publishing Platform)
Romantic Pieces by Frantisek Max Knize for Ukulele (CreateSpace Independent Publishing Platform)
Notebook for Anna Magdalena Bach and Ukulele (CreateSpace Independent Publishing Platform)

For C tuning with low G
Irish tunes for all ukulele (CreateSpace Independent Publishing Platform)
Gospel Ukulele low G Solos (CreateSpace Independent Publishing Platform)
Antonin Dvorak: Biblical Songs: for Ukulele with low G (CreateSpace Independent Publishing Platform)
Gregorian chant for Ukulele with low G (CreateSpace Independent Publishing Platform)
The Czech Lute for Ukulele with low G (CreateSpace Independent Publishing Platform)
Romantic Pieces by Frantisek Max Knize for Ukulele with low G (CreateSpace Independent Publishing Platform)
Notebook for Anna Magdalena Bach and Ukulele with low G (CreateSpace Independent Publishing Platform)

For Baritone ukulele
Irish tunes for all ukulele (CreateSpace Independent Publishing Platform)
Gospel Baritone Ukulele Solos (CreateSpace Independent Publishing Platform)
Antonin Dvorak: Biblical Songs: for Baritone Ukulele (CreateSpace Independent Publishing Platform)
Gregorian chant for Baritone Ukulele (CreateSpace Independent Publishing Platform)
The Czech Lute for Baritone Ukulele (CreateSpace Independent Publishing Platform)
Romantic Pieces by Frantisek Max Knize for Baritone Ukulele (CreateSpace Independent Publishing Platform)
Notebook for Anna Magdalena Bach and Baritone Ukulele (CreateSpace Independent Publishing Platform)

For 6 sting ukulele (Lili'u ukulele)
Gospel 6 string Ukulele Solos (CreateSpace Independent Publishing Platform)
Gregorian chant for 6 string Ukulele (CreateSpace Independent Publishing Platform)
Notebook for Anna Magdalena Bach and 6 string Ukulele (CreateSpace Independent Publishing Platform)

For Slide ukulele (lap steel ukulele)
Comprehensive Slide Ukulele: Guidance for Slide Ukulele Playing (CreateSpace Independent Publishing Platform)
Gospel Slide Ukulele Solos (CreateSpace Independent Publishing Platform)
Irish tunes for slide ukulele (CreateSpace Independent Publishing Platform)

For D tuning ukulele
Skola hry na ukulele (G+W s.r.o.)
Irish tunes for all ukulele (CreateSpace Independent Publishing Platform)

Coming soon!

Jewish songs for ukulele (CreateSpace Independent Publishing Platform)
Notebook for Anna Magdalena Bach: Duet (CreateSpace Independent Publishing Platform)
Open Tunings for Ukulel (Mel Bay Publications)

CPSIA information can be obtained at www.ICGtesting.com
Printed in the USA
LVOW02s1606010814

397113LV00014BA/589/P

9 781481 013192